DISNEY

The following songs are the property of:

Bourne Co.
Music Publishing
5 West 37th Street
New York, NY 10018

BABY MINE
WHEN YOU WISH UPON A STAR
WHISTLE WHILE YOU WORK

ISBN 978-1-4234-8324-3

7777 W. BLUEMOUND RD. P.O. BOX 13819 MILWAUKEE, WI 53213

Visit Hal Leonard Online at
www.halleonard.com

CONTENTS

Beauty and the Beast

Lyrics by Howard Ashman
Music by Alan Menken

Blending traditional animation with computer-generated imagery, this is the only full-length animated feature film ever nominated for an Academy Award for Best Picture and the first film to receive three Academy Award nominations for Best Song, from which this one, sung by Celine Dion and Peabo Bryson, became the Oscar winner.

Hints & Tips: Make sure the eighth notes are rhythmical throughout. Play lyrically with a legato, singing tone.

Baby Mine

Words by Ned Washington
Music by Frank Churchill

This film, based on a book by Helen Aberson, tells the story of Dumbo, an elephant with extraordinarily large ears. This song is sung during Dumbo's visit to his mother's cell, Mrs. Jumbo having been locked up after losing her temper with a group of children who were ridiculing her son.

Hints & Tips: A triplet is a group of three notes, equal in length, which are to be fitted into the time that two notes of the same type would take. Thus the triplet quarter notes in this piece should be played within two beats.

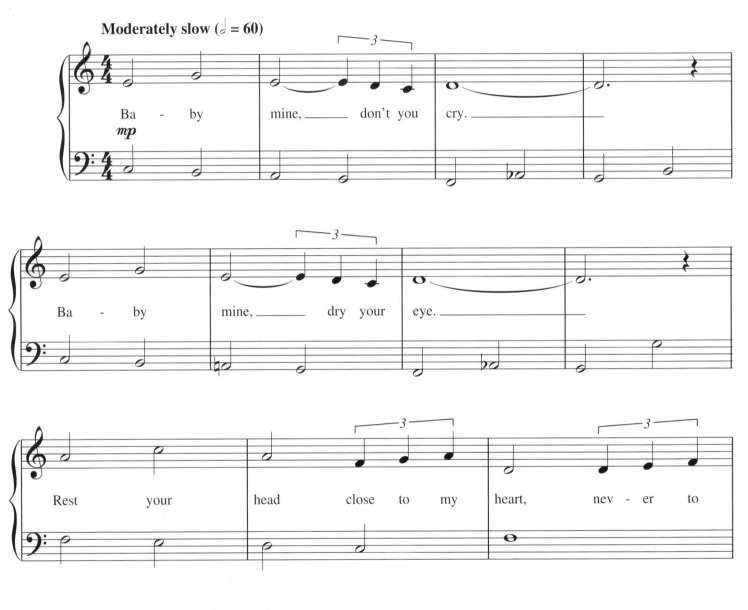

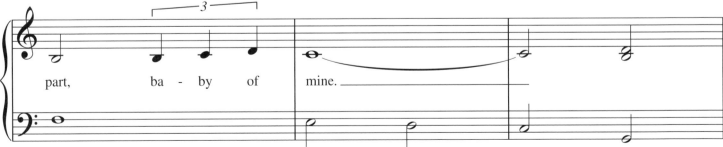

Lit - tle one, _____ when you play, _____

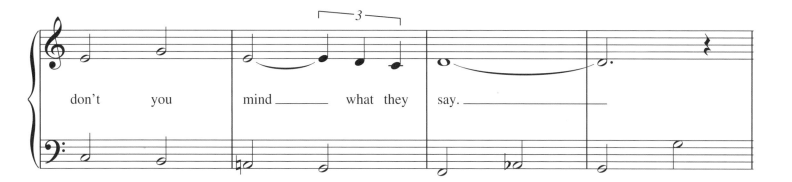

don't you mind _____ what they say. _____

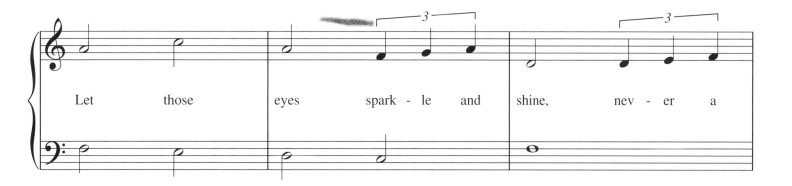

Let those eyes spark - le and shine, nev - er a

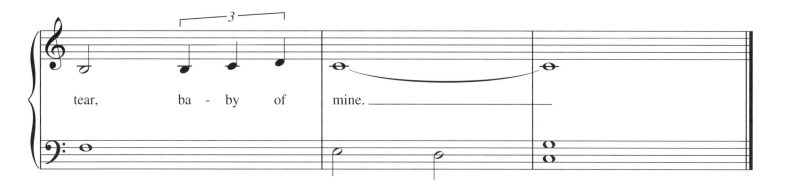

tear, ba - by of mine. _____

from Walt Disney's THE JUNGLE BOOK

The Bare Necessities

Words and Music by
Terry Gilkyson

The Sherman Brothers were enlisted to completely rewrite the music for this animated feature, based on the book of the same name by Rudyard Kipling. Composed by long-time Disney collaborator Terry Gilkyson and sung by characters Baloo and Mowgli, this song was the only track to survive from the earlier, rejected draft.

Hints & Tips: Follow the words of the song to help you with the tied rhythms. 2/2 means two beats per measure, which gives this tune a bouncing, energetic feeling.

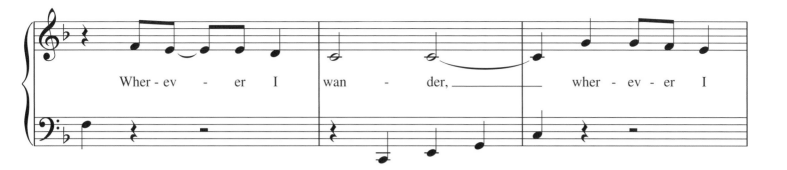

Wher - ev - er I wan - der, _____ wher - ev - er I

roam, _____ I could - n't be fon - der _____

_____ of my big home. _____ The bees are buzz - in' in the

trees to make some hon - ey just for me. The bare ne -

ces - si - ties of life will come to you. _____

Bibbidi-Bobbidi-Boo
(The Magic Song)

Words by Jerry Livingston
Music by Mack David and Al Hoffman

While in New York on business, Walt Disney kept hearing a novelty song, "Chi-Baba Chi-Baba," played on the radio and hired its three composers to write for *Cinderella*. Little surprise then that this similar song appeared in the film and became a hit single, most notably for Perry Como & The Fontane Sisters.

Hints & Tips: Practice the R.H. alone in measures 1-4. Note the triplet rhythms and the accidentals. Plan your fingering. These measures are repeated again in measures 5-8, and again (with a different ending) in measures 13-16.

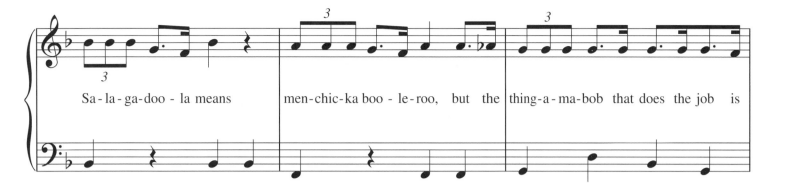

Sa - la - ga - doo - la means men - chic - ka boo - le - roo, but the thing - a - ma - bob that does the job is

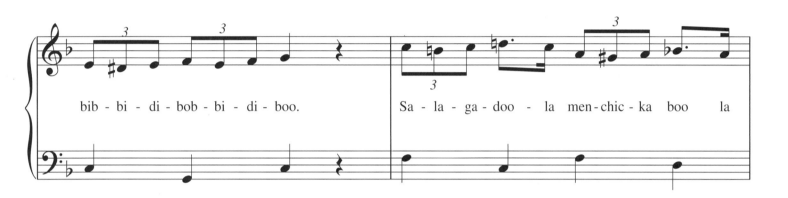

bib - bi - di - bob - bi - di - boo. Sa - la - ga - doo - la men - chic - ka boo la

bib - bi - di - bob - bi - di - boo. Put 'em to - geth - er and what have you got?

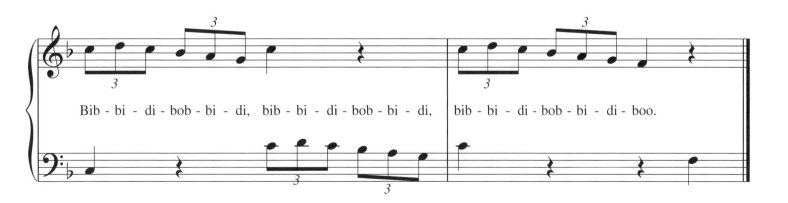

Bib - bi - di - bob - bi - di, bib - bi - di - bob - bi - di, bib - bi - di - bob - bi - di - boo.

Breaking Free

Words and Music by
Jamie Houston

At the climax of what the author describes as a modern adaptation of *Romeo and Juliet*, the main characters, Troy and Gabriella, audition for the winter musical in front of the entire school. Gabriella freezes when she sees everyone staring at her, but encouraged by Troy, she finds the courage to sing this song.

Hints & Tips: The chorus (measures 21-36) should be played with more energy than the rest of the song. Keep the L.H. light and bouncy and make sure the tempo doesn't drag when you get to the tied notes in the R.H. of measures 23-24 and 31-32.

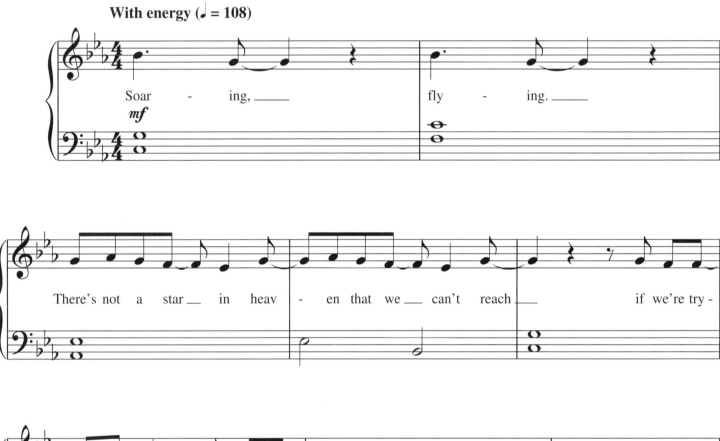

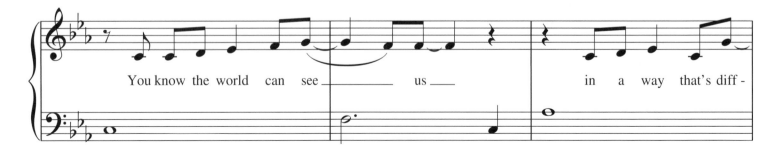

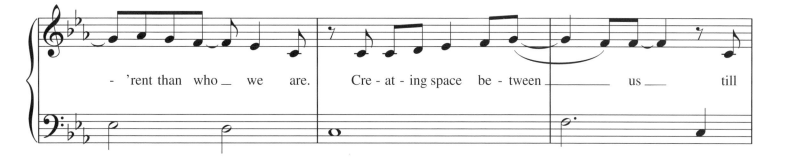

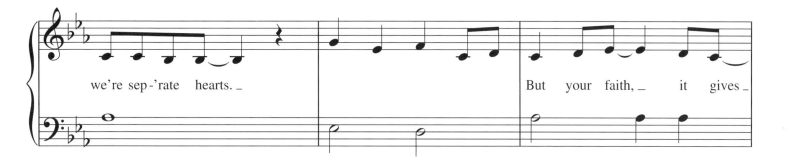

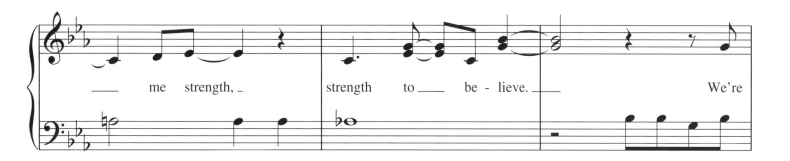

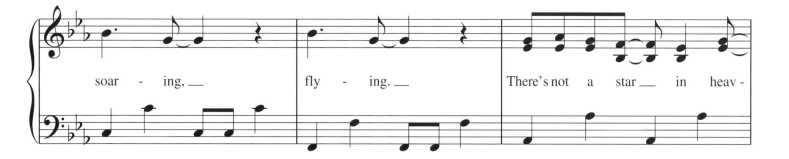

ing free. Oh, we're break - ing free. We're run - ning, _

climb - ing, _ to get to that place, _ to be _ all that we _ can be.

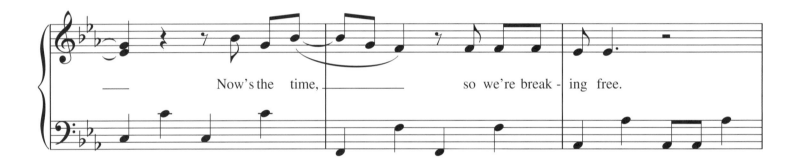

_ Now's the time, _ so we're break - ing free.

Oh. _ We know the world can see _ us

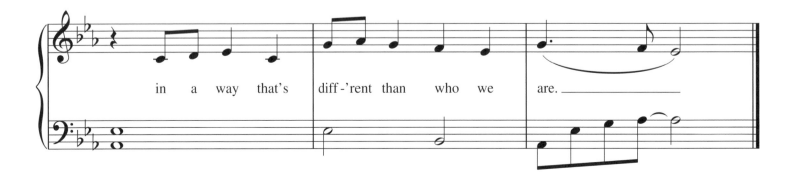

in a way that's diff -'rent than who we are. _

from Walt Disney's THE LITTLE MERMAID
Under the Sea

Music by Alan Menken
Lyrics by Howard Ashman

After a string of critical and commercial failures dating back to the early 1980s, this 1989 film, based on the Hans Christian Andersen fairy tale, is given credit for breathing life back into the animated feature film genre and marked the start of an era known as the Disney Renaissance, or the New Golden Age of Animation.

Hints & Tips: There is a lot of syncopation in this song, creating a calypso feel. Mark in the quarter note beats with a line above the staff if this helps you keep your bearings, particularly in measures 22-23 where the right and left hands should move together.

o - cean floor. Such won - der - ful things sur - round you.

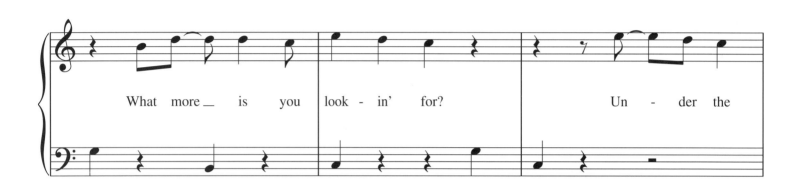

What more __ is you look - in' for? Un - der the

sea, un - der the sea.

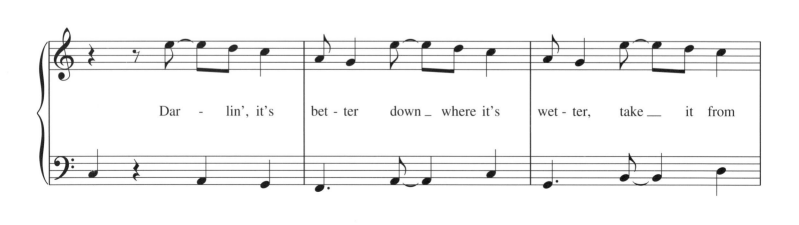

Dar - lin', it's bet - ter down __ where it's wet - ter, take __ it from

me.   Up   on   the   shore they work   all   day;

out   in   the   sun they slave   a - way.   While we   de -

vot - in'   full - time   to   float - in' un - der the   sea.

Can You Feel the Love Tonight

Music by Elton John
Lyrics by Tim Rice

Signed by Disney to write the lyrics for this 1994 animated film and invited to suggest anyone in the world to write the music, Tim Rice selected Elton John. Strongly influenced by Shakespeare's play *Hamlet* and set in the Pride Lands of the Serengeti, the movie tells the story of the relationship between a lion cub and his father.

Hints & Tips: Most of the rhythms and fingering in this piece are straightforward, so take the opportunity to be expressive in your performance—think about phrasing (where to breathe) and dynamics. Listen carefully to the thirds in the right hand of the chorus to ensure the two notes are sounding at exactly the same time.

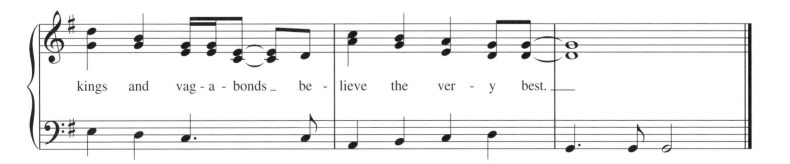

Candle on the Water

Words and Music by Al Kasha
and Joel Hirschhorn

Mocked by her father for her belief that her lover will return after being lost at sea for more than a year, Nora, played by Helen Reddy, sings this ballad from the balcony of the lighthouse in which they live, assuring his spirit that, though he may never return, she will never stop loving him.

Hints & Tips: Practice the chromatic passage in the left hand at measure 24 slowly until you are comfortable with the compacted hand position this phrase requires.

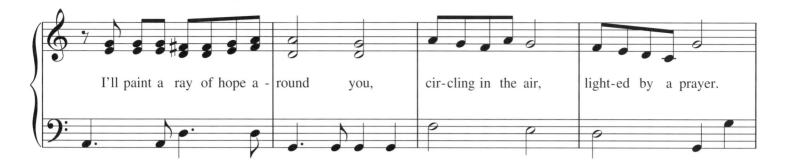

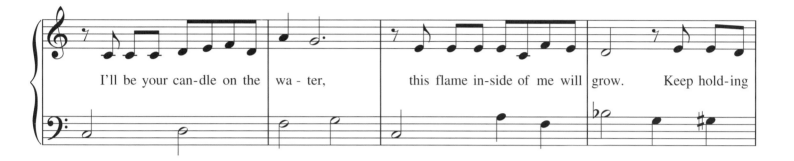

from Walt Disney's MARY POPPINS

Chim Chim Cher-ee

Words and Music by Richard M. Sherman
and Robert B. Sherman

Based on a series of books by P.L. Travers and starring Julie Andrews and Dick Van Dyke, the 1964 musical film *Mary Poppins* is thought by many to be the pinnacle of the Sherman Brothers' decade-long association as staff songwriters at Disney and the crowning achievement in Walt Disney's long career in the film business.

Hints & Tips: Place an emphasis on the first beat in each measure, especially in the left hand, to create a strong waltz feel to this jolly song.

Chim chim-i-ney, chim chim-i-ney, chim chim che-ree. A

sweep is as luck-y as luck-y can be.

Chim chim-i-ney, chim chim-i-ney, chim chim che-roo. Good

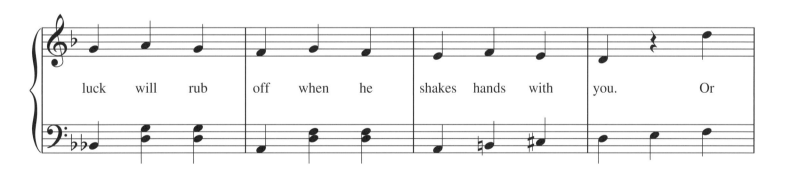

luck will rub off when he shakes hands with you. Or

blow me a kiss, and that's luck-y, too.

The Climb

Words and Music by Jessi Alexander
and Jon Mabe

This ballad, from the 2009 musical adaptation of the teen sitcom, laments the struggles of the double life led by Miley Stewart as Hannah Montana, her popstar alter-ego. Home in Tennessee, Miley, played by Miley Cyrus, reconnects with a childhood friend and soon realizes that her family life has been neglected.

Hints & Tips: Avoid heavy-sounding L.H. chords by placing a slight emphasis on the first beat of each measure and playing the remaining three beats more softly. Play the two notes at exactly the same time.

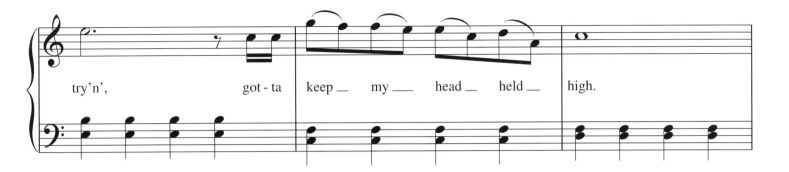

try'n', got-ta keep my head held high.

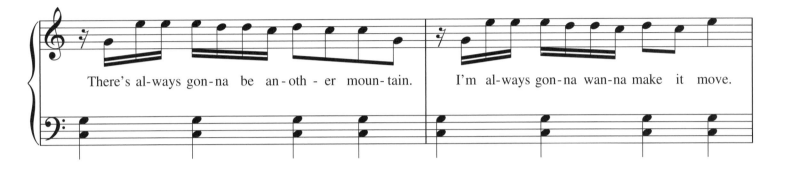

There's al-ways gon-na be an-oth-er moun-tain. I'm al-ways gon-na wan-na make it move.

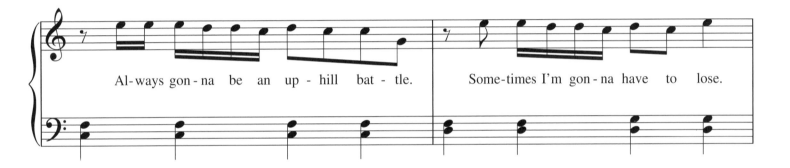

Al-ways gon-na be an up-hill bat-tle. Some-times I'm gon-na have to lose.

Ain't a-bout how fast I get there. Ain't a-bout what's wait-ing on the oth-er

side. It's the climb.

Colors of the Wind

Music by Alan Menken
Lyrics by Stephen Schwartz

This was the first Disney animated feature to be based on a real historical character, namely the Native American woman, Pocahontas. It portrays a fictionalized account of her encounter with English settlers to whom, in this song, she tries to explain the wonders of the earth and nature, including the spirit within all living things.

Hints & Tips: Rather than keeping strictly to the tempo as you play this piece, achieve a relaxed, wistful feel by employing *rubato*. This means you "give and take," moving forward with the tempo at times and holding back with the tempo at other times.

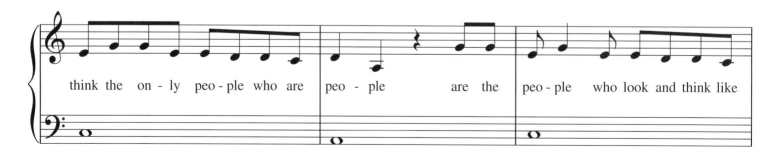

you, but if you walk the foot-steps of a strang - er, you'll learn

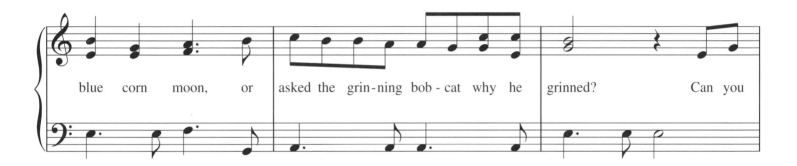

things you nev - er knew you nev - er knew. Have you ev - er heard the wolf cry to the

blue corn moon, or asked the grin-ning bob - cat why he grinned? Can you

sing with all the voic - es of the moun - tain? Can you paint with all the col - ors of the

wind? Can you paint with all the col - ors of the wind?

from Walt Disney Pictures' ENCHANTED

Happy Working Song

Music by Alan Menken
Lyrics by Stephen Schwartz

In this 2007 homage to conventional Disney-animated features, Giselle, an archetypal Disney princess, is forced from her traditional, animated Kingdom of Andalasia into the live-action world of New York City where urban vermin such as pigeon, rats, and cockroaches respond to her call for help with the cleaning.

Hints & Tips: This song is based almost entirely on the C major scale. If you practice this scale, both hands separately and together, you will soon find the melodic movement required in this piece much easier, as well as the slower-moving accompanying line.

kit - chen as we sing a - long.

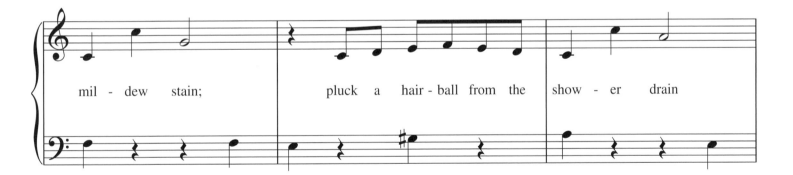

Trill a cheer - y tune in the tub as you scrub a stub - born

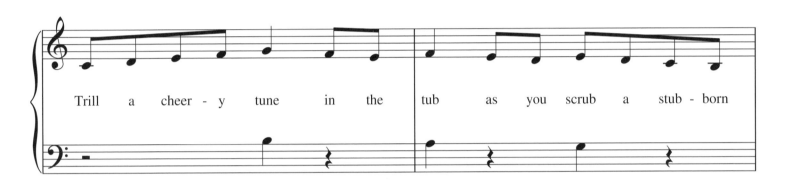

mil - dew stain; pluck a hair - ball from the show - er drain

to the gay re - frain of a hap - py work - ing song.

If I Didn't Have You

Music and Lyrics by
Randy Newman

After 15 nominations without a win, Randy Newman finally landed his first Oscar when this song, from the computer-animated comedy about a city of paranoid monsters who generate power from the screams of children, won the Academy Award for Best Original Song.

Hints & Tips: Play this song with a swing feel by making the first eighth note in each pair slightly longer than the second. Try to listen to the original recording if you are unsure how this will sound.

I would-n't have noth-in' if I did-n't have you. Would-n't have

noth-in' if I did-n't have, ____ would-n't have

noth-in' if I did-n't have, ____ would-n't have

noth-in'... ____ you.

Little April Shower

Words by Larry Morey
Music by Frank Churchill

The main characters in this 1942 animated feature film, based on the book *Bambi, A Life in the Woods* by Austrian author Felix Salten, are Bambi, a white-tailed deer, his parents, his friends Thumper (a rabbit) and Flower (a skunk), and his future mate Faline.

Hints & Tips: Note the key change at measure 9—there are now four sharps: F♯, C♯, G♯, and D♯. In measure 17, the key changes back to C Major.

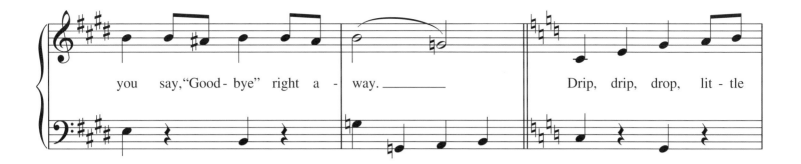

you say, "Good-bye" right a - way. _____ Drip, drip, drop, lit - tle

A - pril show - er, beat - ing a tune as you fall all a - round. Drip, drip, drop, lit - tle

A - pril show - er, what can com - pare with your beau - ti - ful sound.

Drip, drop, drip, drop. I'll nev - er be a - fraid of a

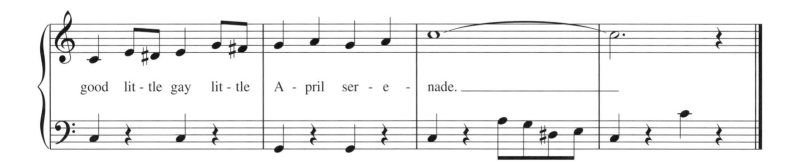

good lit - tle gay lit - tle A - pril ser - e - nade. _____

Someone's Waiting for You

Words by Carol Connors and Ayn Robbins
Music by Sammy Fain

Based on children's novels by Margery Sharp, *The Rescuers* tells the story of an international mouse organization dedicated to helping victims of abduction around the world, which, like the United Nations, has headquarters in New York. This song plays while such a victim is comforted by a shining star.

Hints & Tips: Keep the left hand relatively quiet as it bubbles along beneath the melody in this arrangement. Keep your wrist loose and rock gently between the notes.

till your hopes and your wish - es come true.

You must try to be brave lit - tle one.____

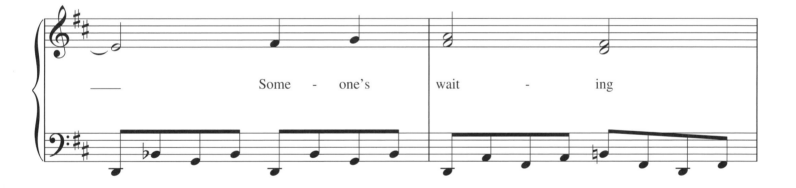

____ Some - one's wait - ing

to love you.____

from Walt Disney Pictures' TOY STORY 2 - A Pixar Film

When She Loved Me

Music and Lyrics by
Randy Newman

The 1999 sequel to *Toy Story* again featured the secret adventures of a group of toys. Performed by Sarah McLachlan, this song is used for a flashback montage in which Jessie, a yodelling cowgirl, experiences being loved, forgotten, and finally abandoned by her owner Emily.

Hints & Tips: Think about the story this song tells and try to convey this in your performance using dynamics and rubato. Sing through the song to help determine the phrasing you will use.

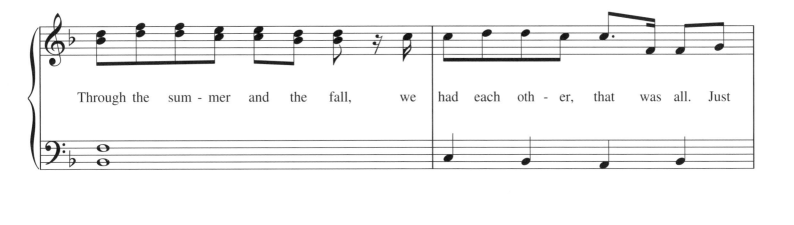

Through the sum - mer and the fall, we had each oth - er, that was all. Just

she and I to - geth - er, like it was meant to be.

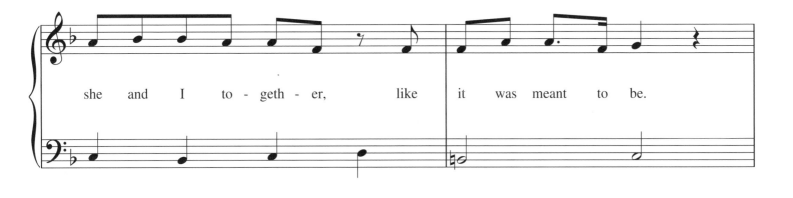

And when she was lone - ly, I was there to com-fort her, and I knew_____ that

she loved me.

from Walt Disney's PINOCCHIO

When You Wish Upon a Star

Words by Ned Washington
Music by Leigh Harline

Sung by the character Jiminy Cricket, at #7, this is the highest-ranked Disney song on the American Film Institute's list of 100 Greatest Songs In Film History. The first seven notes of the melody have become an icon of the Walt Disney Company, even being adopted as the horn signal of the ships of the Disney Cruise Line.

Hints & Tips: Practice this piece slowly at first. This will help steer you through the numerous accidentals and the often unusual intervals between notes.

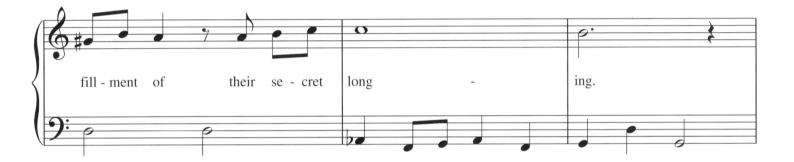

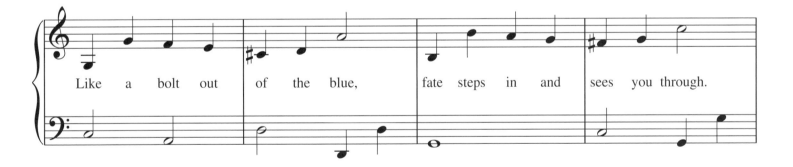

Whistle While You Work

Words by Larry Morey
Music by Frank Churchill

Following on the success of their *Silly Symphonies* cartoon series, in 1937 Walt Disney Studios made this, their first full-length animated feature, based on the fairy tale of the same name by the Brothers Grimm, beginning what is now considered to be the Golden Age of Disney Animation which lasted until the early 1940s.

Hints & Tips: Give the phrases in this song shape by placing a slight emphasis on the first beat in each measure. Be sure to observe the rests in the left hand to create a light, bouncy feel throughout.

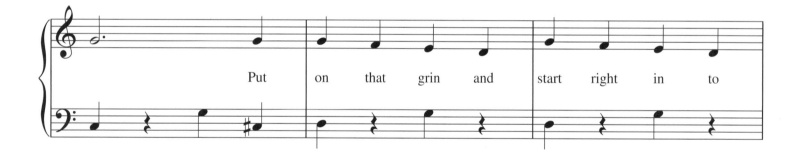

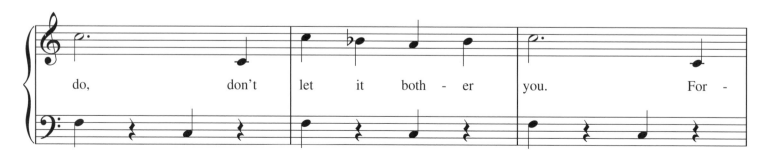

get your trou - bles,   try to be just   like a cheer - ful

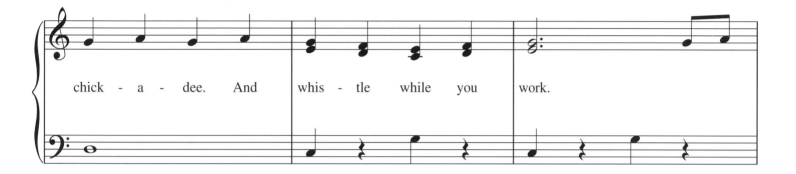

chick - a - dee. And   whis - tle while you   work.

Come   on, get smart, tune

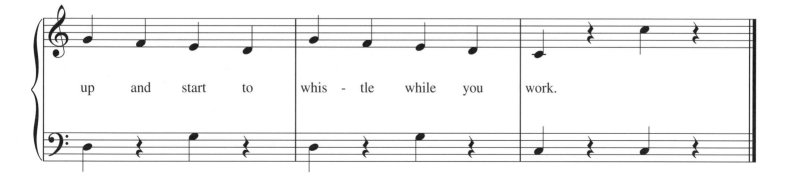

up and start to   whis - tle while you   work.

from Walt Disney's ALADDIN
A Whole New World

Music by Alan Menken
Lyrics by Tim Rice

Tim Rice took over as lyricist for this movie, based on the Arabian folk tale "Aladdin's Wonderful Lamp" from *One Thousand and One Nights*, when Disney regular Howard Ashman died in early 1991. In 1993 this became the first Disney song ever to reach #1 on the US *Billboard* Hot 100.

Hints & Tips: Don't forget that the key signature is F Major, which means there are B♭s to remember. Also notice that the left hand has an interesting moving part in measures 10 and 18.

view. No one to tell us no, or where to go, or

say we're on - ly dream - ing. A whole new world, ____

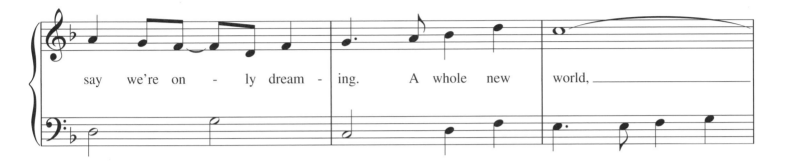

____ a daz - zling place I nev - er knew. But when I'm

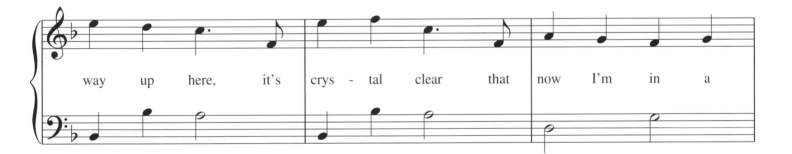

way up here, it's crys - tal clear that now I'm in a

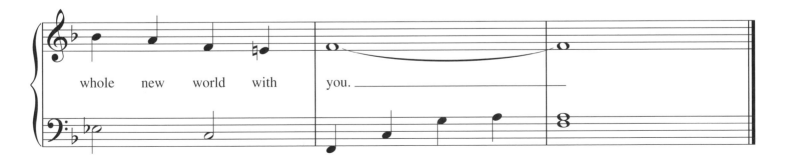

whole new world with you. ____

from Walt Disney Pictures' TARZAN ™

You'll Be in My Heart

Words and Music by
Phil Collins

Based on Edgar Rice Burroughs' book, *Tarzan of the Apes*, this 1999 animated feature is about a man raised by gorillas who has to decide where he truly belongs when he discovers he is a human. In this song the adoptive mother gorilla, Kala, sings that Tarzan should stop crying because she will keep him safe and warm.

Hints & Tips: Imagine the left hand part is being played by an African drum, its steady rhythm underpinning the melody. Use a metronome to maintain a consistent tempo.

can't be bro - ken.   I will be here; don't you cry.   'Cause   you'll be   in   my

heart.   Yes, you'll be   in   my   heart.   From this day   on, —

now and for - ev - er   more.   You'll be   in   my

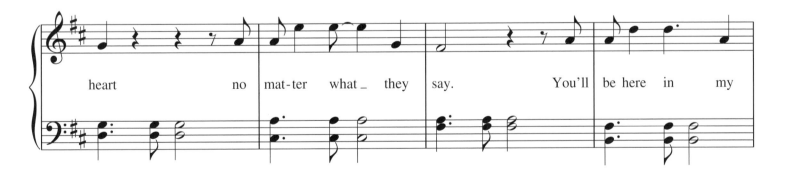

heart   no mat-ter what — they   say.   You'll be here in   my

heart   al - ways.

from Walt Disney's TOY STORY

You've Got a Friend in Me

Music and Lyrics by
Randy Newman

Composer Randy Newman established his trademark Pixar Animation Studios sound in this 1995 film about the secret life of toys when people are not around; particularly that of cowboy Woody and Buzz Lightyear, a space ranger. It was the first full-length feature film to use only computer-generated imagery.

Hints & Tips: Play this piece with a gentle swing to capture the laid-back feel of the song, but don't become too relaxed—there are plenty of accidentals to keep an eye out for!

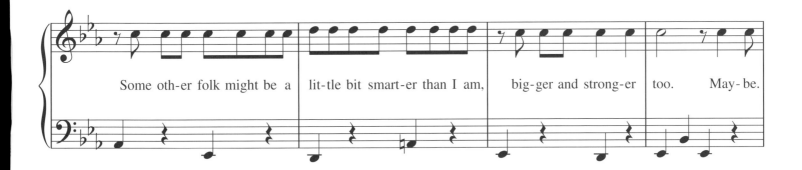

Some oth-er folk might be a lit-tle bit smart-er than I am, big-ger and strong-er too. May-be.

But none of them will ev - er love you the way I do, __ just me and you.

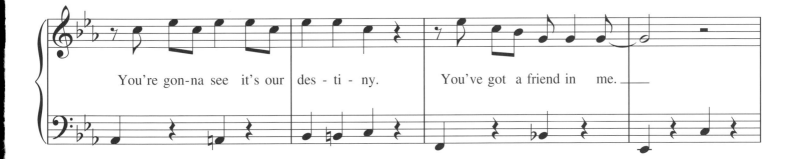

And as the years go by, __ our friend-ship will nev - er die. __

You're gon-na see it's our des - ti - ny. You've got a friend in me. __

You've got a friend in me. __ You've got a friend in me. __

from Walt Disney Pictures' HERCULES

Zero to Hero

Music by Alan Menken
Lyrics by David Zippel

Greek mythology became a new source of inspiration for Disney studios in this 1997 animated feature which tells the story of Hercules, son of Zeus, who is kidnapped by the evil Hades, Lord of the Underworld. Drained of all powers bar his strength, he becomes a hero by battling various monsters sent to destroy him.

Hints & Tips: This up-tempo gospel number should have real pizzazz, but try not to rush. Instead, listen carefully to be sure the left and right hand notes sound at exactly the same time, particularly where there is eighth note movement in the left hand, for example, bars 3, 7, 13, 15 and 17.

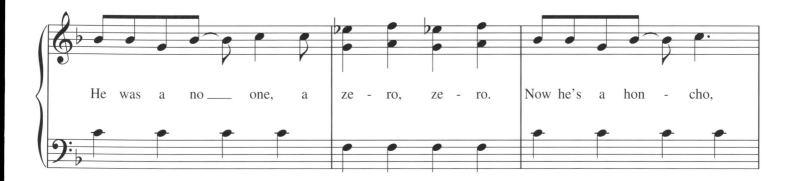

He was a no — one, a ze - ro, ze - ro. Now he's a hon - cho,

he's a he - ro. Here was a kid — with his act down pat. From

ze - ro to he - ro in no ——— time ——— flat.

Ze - ro to he - ro just like that.

from Walt Disney's SONG OF THE SOUTH

Zip-A-Dee-Doo-Dah

Words by Ray Gilbert
Music by Allie Wrubel

This upbeat tune from the 1946 movie, based on the Uncle Remus stories about the adventures of Br'er Rabbit and his friends, was sung by James Baskett. He received an honorary Academy Award for his performance 18 months after the film's release, becoming the first man of African descent to win an Oscar.

Hints & Tips: Consider playing this short piece twice, employing a quieter dynamic (*p*) the second time through and thus creating a contrast. Employ a crescendo in measures 9-12 leading into the jubilant ending.

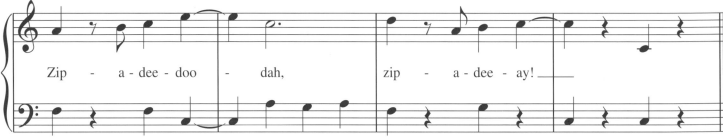